ANIMAL RHYME TIME!

RHYME TIME WITH MONKEYS!

BY JONAS EDWARDS

Gareth Stevens
PUBLISHING

Please visit our website, www.garethstevens.com. For a free color catalog of all our high-quality books, call toll free 1-800-542-2595 or fax 1-877-542-2596.

Library of Congress Cataloging-in-Publication Data

Names: Edwards, Jonas, author.
Title: Rhyme time with monkeys! / Jonas Edwards.
Description: New York : Gareth Stevens Publishing, [2021] | Series: Animal
   rhyme time! | Includes index.
Identifiers: LCCN 2020000855 | ISBN 9781538255964 (library binding) | ISBN
   9781538255940 (paperback) | ISBN 9781538255957 (6 Pack) | ISBN 9781538255971
   (ebook)
Subjects: LCSH: Monkeys–Juvenile literature.
Classification: LCC QL737.P9 E39 2021 | DDC 599.8–dc23
LC record available at https://lccn.loc.gov/2020000855

First Edition

Published in 2021 by
Gareth Stevens Publishing
111 East 14th Street, Suite 349
New York, NY 10003

Editor: Kate Mikoley

Photo credits: Cover, p. 1 OlgaOzik/Shutterstock.com; cover, pp. 3–24 (music notes) StockSmartStart/ Shutterstock.com; p. 5 Goskova Tatiana/Shutterstock.com; p. 7 Theo Allofs/ Corbis Documentary / Getty Images Plus; p. 9 Sean Caffrey/ Lonely Planet Images/ Getty Images Plus; p. 11 Peter Knig / 500px/Getty Images; p. 13 (left) Doug Cheeseman/ Photolibrary / Getty Images Plus; p. 13 (right) avstraliavasin/ iStock / Getty Images Plus; p. 15 Ben Cranke/ Oxford Scientific / Getty Images Plus; p. 17 Eric Gevaert/Shutterstock.com; p. 19 Jenhung Huang/ iStock / Getty Images Plus; p. 21 Per-Gunnar Ostby/ Oxford Scientific/ Getty Images Plus.

Printed in the United States of America

Some of the images in this book illustrate individuals who are models. The depictions do not imply actual situations or events.

CPSIA compliance information: Batch #CS20GS: For further information contact Gareth Stevens, New York, New York at 1-800-542-2595.

Find us on

CONTENTS

Meet the Monkeys 4

Tails and Songs 6

On the Move 8

Worldly Monkeys 10

Smart Animals 14

Monkeying Around 16

The Littlest Monkey 18

Bye Monkeys! 20

Glossary 22

For More Information 23

Index 24

Boldface words appear in the glossary.

Meet the Monkeys

Look! There's a monkey in that tree!

It's a **primate** like you and me.

Monkeys come in many species,

or kinds.

They have big brains and **clever** minds.

There are more monkey facts to learn.

Come along! There's a monkey at

every turn!

Tails and Songs

All monkeys have tails, short or long.

Some monkeys make a loud noise

like a song.

A howler monkey's sound travels

for miles.

As for its tail, it's prehensile.

This means it can be used to grab

or lift.

Not every monkey has this gift.

HOWLER MONKEY

On the Move

Most monkeys live in forests among the trees,
jumping from one branch to another with **ease**.
Monkeys use both of their arms and legs to get around.
They mainly walk on all fours when traveling on the ground.

Worldly Monkeys

There are two main kinds of monkeys on Earth.

You can tell what kind one is by its place of birth.

Africa and Asia are where Old World monkeys are from.

They include macaques and baboons, to name some.

BABOONS

11

New World monkeys are the second kind.

Check South America up to Mexico if they're what you want to find.

Old World monkeys have **nostrils** that are close together.

New World monkeys' nostrils are far apart, however.

NEW WORLD MONKEY

OLD WORLD MONKEY

13

Smart Animals

Monkeys learn by doing things, just like people do.

Most monkeys know how to figure out **difficult** problems too.

Some monkeys know how to use objects as tools.

A stone can be used to open nuts—it's not against the monkey rules!

Monkeying Around

Monkeys are social animals and live in groups.

They look for food together in these groups, called troops.

Troops can have a thousand monkeys or just a few.

Adults carry babies when they're not playing with their crew.

The Littlest Monkey

The world's smallest monkey is the size of a banana. Did you know?
But its tail is longer than its body from head to toe!
These tiny monkeys are called pygmy marmosets.
Some people want one, but monkeys aren't pets!

Bye Monkeys!

Monkeys belong to a group of animals known as **mammals**.

Other kinds of mammals include humans, dogs, and camels.

Many great animals live in the wild, you see,

but monkeys are the best of the best if you ask me!

GLOSSARY

clever: showing intelligent, or smart, thinking

difficult: hard to do

ease: lack of difficulty

mammal: a warm-blooded animal that has a backbone and hair, breathes air, and feeds milk to its young

nostril: an opening through which an animal breathes

primate: any animal from the group that includes humans, apes, and monkeys

FOR MORE INFORMATION

BOOKS

Moses, Brian. *Animal Poems*. New York, NY: Windmill Books, 2018.

Murray, Julie. *Monkeys*. Minneapolis, MN: Big Buddy Books, 2020.

Randolph, Joanne. *Poems About Animals*. New York, NY: Windmill Books, 2019.

WEBSITES

Howler Monkey

kids.nationalgeographic.com/animals/mammals/howler-monkey/
Learn more about howler monkeys here.

Monkey

animals.sandiegozoo.org/animals/monkey
Head to the San Diego Zoo's website to find out more about monkeys.

Monkeys

www.dkfindout.com/us/animals-and-nature/primates/monkeys
Check out this website for more facts about monkeys.

INDEX

Africa 10

Asia 10

baboon 10, 11

howler monkey 6, 7

macaque 10

mammal 20

Mexico 12

New World monkey 12, 13

nostril 12

Old World monkey 10, 12, 13

prehensile 6

primate 4

pygmy marmoset 18

South America 12

species 4

tail 6, 18

troop 16